Killer Cop: Unnecessary Use of Deadly Physical Force and How to protect yourself from being shot

I0476191

By Sherman Williams

Table of Contents

Foreword

Every government around the word has the mandate of providing security to its citizens. This is always possible though putting in place effective and efficient law enforcement measures and apparatus. The question is: what becomes of the safety of citizens, which a government seeks to provide, when incidences of police brutality have increased in recent times and many lives have been lost more even than the number terrorism claims in a year? The United States of America is a home to at least 130 million people. Of this population, at least 50 million are African Americans. In recent memory, incidences of unarmed civilians shot and killed by police have hit headlines around the world. This has cast into light a deeply rooted American problem and as a result has brought to focus, the history of the slave trade in America when blacks were considered savages and treated to brutal servitude. Racism was the means by which opportunities were distributed, legal processes applied and access to public utilities granted. Could it be that the vice of racism still exists amidst peace-loving and united Americans? Or could it be that the police are being militarized for security reasons? Many people have been killed by cops on American soil but those viewed by the public as racially instigated, have always sparked relentless and widespread public protests.

When news of a white policeman who has shot and killed a black teenager makes headlines in the US, it goes viral around the world and the welfare of people living in a country that has played very instrumental and appreciable roles in maintaining world peace becomes a big debate.

Studies have unearthed implicit and explicit racially propagated crimes, committed by both the police and civilians. There have also been cases of a black policemen shooting and killing unarmed white civilians but this has not always made headlines around the world compared to incidences of white police officers shooting and killing teenage African Americans.

In the practice of law enforcement as well as maintenance of peace and order, citizens of a country have always put their faith in the police. Even though there have been unfortunate and even intentional incidences of armed civilians shooting and killing cops in America the magnitude of the problem is always highlighted when a Cop uses excessive force when arresting suspected law breakers and wanted criminals. We are then fast forwarded to a generation of suspicion and overt racism. Civilians no longer believe the police can protect them and as a result seek to acquire a firearm by any means for self-protection or to partake in criminal activities. Incidentally, research has established that the amount of firearms owned by civilians is many times more than firearms owned by the police forces around the world combined. This complicates the whole problem. Killer Cops have more often than not attributed their shoot to kill civilians to an act of self-defense. To them, the civilians that have been taken down by bullets were armed and dangerous. The aggrieved parties have always spotted foul play in such allegations given the fact that some video recordings have shown that citizens who have been killed by cops were actually not armed and dangerous as purported by police. This brings to the fore what needs to be done in light of perceived racial shootings and asks the question: are the police actually threatened despite the training they have undergone when it comes to law and order enforcement? Is the police department violating its own established codes of conduct?

Introduction

The United States of America has a long history—dating back to over two hundred years—of law enforcement and policing. Credited as a world power, what quickly comes to mind is that America is well-protected both internally and externally. But what do you make of America's homeland security when the term Killer Cop traces its origin to incidences of America's law enforcement officers who have been accused of shooting and killing unarmed civilians? The trend is even more worrying because almost all incidents of Killer Cops killing unarmed civilians have been linked to racism.

Statistics reported by the Federal Bureau of Investigation (FBI), have brought to the fore shocking revelations and thwarted the thinking that only African Americans are targeted. According to FBI findings, just like many African Americans have lost their lives at the hands of white killer cops , so have white Americans lost their lives in the hands of black killer cops. Incidences of armed civilians killing police officers have also hit headlines. However, what has raised eyebrows even beyond the America's borders is a disturbing truth. Despite evidence gathered showing that at least 95% of those who have had their lives ended at the hands of killer cops were unarmed and therefore not dangerous, investigations into these killings have always seen the killer cops set free. This has more often than not brought to fore the conduct of police officers. Allegations of police militarization have remained largely speculative.

In less than two decades, many black teenagers and a number of white teenagers have lost their lives thanks to the use of deadly force by police officers. Fear continues to grip many who believe that this trend is likely to escalate if something urgent is not done.

With a legal system that has always appeared skewed in favor of the police, killer cops have walked away free. It has been a case of justice denied. This brings us to another big question: how many blacks have been killed by American homeland security officers? Well, the number is undoubtedly higher than what has been recorded in court files save for those who were killed but their fate never made it into the news headlines. One asks; is the media skewed in its coverage of killer cop incidences? In chapter one, we delve into names of those who have been killed by police in America and especially African Americans. Please ensure you take note of the circumstances, as reported by police that led to their deaths.

Chapter 1: Killer Cop: Tracing the history of Minority (Black) Killings in the U.S.A by Police

In this chapter, we take an insightful look into the number of African Americans whose lives have been ended by police gunfire because this is what has made headlines around the world and appears to reignite America's long struggle with racism as well as what some people now call racially instigated killings. Also, a look into a few isolated cases of police shootings and killings of white civilians would add an invaluable and insightful understanding of deadly force as used by police against unarmed civilians.

Unarmed African Americans slain by Killer Cops

Here, we take a look at landmark cases and incidences of African Americans who what been killed by White Cops.

Rumain Brisbon

Rumain was aged 34 and a father of four at the time he was shot and killed by a cop in Arizona. It was alleged that the police officer who shot and killed Rumain mistook the bottle of pills he was carrying for a gun. Following the fatal shooting of Rumain which ended his life on December 2nd in 2014, tens of thousands of protestors took to the streets sand staged a march that saw them reach Phoenix police headquarters to demand the release of the name of the cop who shot and killed Rumain. A police spokesman was reported to have defended the act by saying the killer cop did what was expected of him.

Police reports indicated that at the time of Brisbon's death, news of a drug deal in the areas had put the cops on high alert and that the substance was carried in a black SUV.

Brisbon was at the time taking something out of the trunk of his black SUV and when the police approached him, Brisbon, according to police reports, tried to escape after ignoring orders to raise his hands. His hands were also in his waistband and this prompted a police officer who was said to be thirty years of age and with seven years' experience in the service to draw his gun. The cop was reported to have wrestled Brisbon down and a struggle ensued. When on the ground, according to police spokesman Trent Crump, Brisbon further ignored an order to keep his hands in his pockets. The cop who held him down is reported to have felt something like the handle of a gun. During the struggle, a woman in a nearby apartment reportedly opened her door. Brisbon and the police reportedly tumbled inside to a back bedroom where two children aged 9 and 12 were sleeping. Police reports further indicated that since the cop could not keep up with the struggle of holding Brisbon's hands in position, the officer shot Brisbon twice in fear of the suspect drawing a firearm he allegedly had in his pocket. Brisbon died on the spot and despite police reports indicating that he had marijuana and a handgun in the boot of his SUV; findings indicated that Brisbon only had a bottle of oxycodone pills at the time of his murder.

- **Tamir Rice**

Rice is another African American whose life ended in Cleveland, Ohio by a killer cop on November 22nd in 2014. The death of Rice took place within seconds on a Saturday afternoon. A cop is alleged to have spotted Rice with a BB gun in the parking lot of Cudell Recreation Center. Further reports indicated that a concerned civilian who spotted Rice with the toy gun tried to call 911. The concerned civilian who called 911 recounted seeing Rice on a swing pulling out the toy gun from his pants and pointing at people with it and putting it back but the civilian was not sure whether it was real gun. On arrival, the police shot at Rice after he refused orders to put up his hands. He was rushed to the hospital but pronounced dead Sunday morning. Rice's family urged demonstrators to be peaceful and remain calm. The family requested the matter to be made public.

- **Akai Gurley**

Gurley was shot by a cop in New York's Brooklyn in a dark stairwell of one of the city's housing project buildings. The officer who shot him, Peter Liang was said to be unaware of what happened. Even his girlfriend and the cop who was standing behind Liang recorded their statements saying they didn't know what happened. Police commissioner William Bratton and Mayor Bill de Blassio termed Gurley as a total innocent. They said the incident was a tragic accident and called for an investigation. Brooklyn attorney Kenneth Thompson brushed aside calls for an independent prosecution saying he is capable of conducting a free and fair investigation.

- **Kajieme Powell**

A 911 call was to end the life of Powell when police officers who responded claimed that the deceased approached them holding a knife but video footage showed that Powell did not come as close to the cops as alleged and that he had no knife. He was shot within 15 seconds of the cops' arrival. Powell, a black man, died at age 25 in St. Louis, Mo on August 19th 2014. Powell, who was said to have a mental illness, was allegedly shot after acting erratically according to the police report and refusing to obey orders. While the video footage that was recorded by an eye witness using a cell phone shows Powell moving towards the cops and being shot at 3 foot range, there is no evidence that the victim had a knife when he met his death. Parents of Powell sued the St. Louis police chief and arresting officers for wrongful death.

- **Ezell Ford**

The death of Ford who was at the time aged 25 is one of those that will linger on in the public domain as a racially targeted killer cop incident.

Ford met his death in hands of cops who were allegedly conducting an investigative stop on 12th August 2014. Parents of the deceased recorded a statement saying their son was lying down at the time he was shot and killed, an indication that he had complied with police orders. The Los Angeles Police Department has since put the investigations on hold. The killing of Ford sparked widespread protests, civilian-police confrontations and looting. Ford was said to be mentally impaired and his mother during an interview at the scene of crime, described him as a good kid who did not have to die the way he did.

- **Dante Parker**

The death of Parker, an African American is one of those that yet again pitted police against the anger of civilians residing in San Bernardino County in California. Parker was shot by cops on the 12th of August 2014, the same day Ford was shot. In what many described as a mistaken identity, police responded to a 911 call about a robbery and the suspect was said to have fled on a bicycle according to eyewitnesses. However, on arrival, Parker was found nearby riding his bicycle. Reports indicated that he was unarmed but when the police tried to arrest him, a resistance struggle ensued. The cops stunned him with a Taser severely, killing him on the spot. At the time of his death, Parker was aged 36. He was working with the Daily Press. His family and friends described him as a likeable person with a great sense of humor. Parker is said to have developed a liking for riding his bicycle in an attempt to lose weight. Parker was also said to have always taken good care of his family of five children.

- **Michael Brown**

In the history of Killer cops taking the lives of black civilians, the shooting of Michael Brown is one of those that sparked widespread outrage and protests. Michael Brown was shot and killed by Officer Daren Wilson when a struggle is alleged to have ensued inside the cop's patrol car.

In his defense, Daren Wilson said Michael looked like a demon. Aged 18 at the time he was shot by Daren Wilson, the death of Brown elicited widespread reactions especially with regard to police killings of teenagers. Brown was said to be unarmed at the time he was shot.

An official report on the investigations into circumstances surrounding Brown's death indicated that Brown was shot at his hand and that there were traces of marijuana in his blood according to autopsy findings. Brown's death in the hands of a killer cop came three days before Parker's and Fords' who were also fatally shot and killed by police. The police officer, Daren Wilson has since resigned from the Ferguson police force. Even today, Ferguson, Missouri protests that ensued after the news of Brown's death have remained a bench mark for increasing cases of killer cops taking away the lives of unarmed civilians.

- **John Crawford III**

On August 5th 2014, just four days before Brown was slain by a killer cop, Crawford, an African American had his life ended by a fatal police shooting. He was shot while carrying a pellet gun in a Wal-Mart. Reports indicates that the gun was not yet sold but has been removed from its casing. A 911 call by a man who was to become known as Ronald Ritchie told the police that Crawford appeared to be pointing the gun at people, only to retract his statement a month later saying Crawford was not pointing at people with the gun. Video footage showed police shooting and killing Crawford in Ohio's Wal-Mat. In their defense, police justified their action citing Crawford's failure to obey commands that required him to put the gun down. He was pronounced dead minutes after arrival at the hospital. It later emerged that apart from Crawford's shooting, a woman named Angela Williams also died from the incident due to heart attack. What Crawford was holding later turned out to be an air rifle that can fire pellets and shoot BBs. At the time of his death, Crawford was aged 22 and left behind a wife and two kids.

- **Tyree Woodson**

Two days before Crawford could meet his death, a Killer Cop had taken the life of 38 years old Tyree in Baltimore. However, according to the police, Woodson died from a fatally self-inflicted gunshot. It was alleged that Woodson smuggled a high caliber gun into a police station to commit the crime in order to bring a case against his accusers. Woodson was said to have multiple police arrest warrants. Many questions remained unanswered as to how Baltimore police could arrest someone considered violent and bring him to custody without noticing he was carrying a gun. With many people including Woodson's mother who read mischief into the circumstances surrounding his death, there is still much controversy and mystery surrounding the death of Woodson even as investigations have yet to unravel the truth. His family, while acknowledging that their son was violent, argued that he ought to have been frisked before being put in a holding cell.

- **Eric Garner**

On the 17th of July 2014, residents of New York City were yet again treated to what many would later call a killer cop taking away a black life. This time however, the victim did not succumb to a gunshot wound but to a chokehold. The New York Police Department alleged in their report that Eric Garner, who died aged 43, was selling illegal and untaxed cigars contrary to witness accounts that Garner was stopped by NYPD after he broke up a fight. An argument was to ensue during which NYPD cop Daniel Pantaleo put Garner in a chokehold. Unfortunately, the hold was long enough to take Garner's life due to neck and chest compression. A medical examiner based in New York ruled that Garner's death was a homicide. The officer was not brought to justice.

A Case of Undocumented Blacks Slain by Killer Cops.

Apart from the African Americans whose deaths have taken place in the hands of cops due to use of deadly force and in the event sparking public outrage and protests, there are hundreds others that have escaped the public eye either because the matter was justifiable or because the media did not give any coverage.

Talking of black killer cops victims like Amadou Diallo (1999), Malcolm Ferguson (2000), Patrick Dorismon (2000), Ronald Beasley and Earl Murray (2000), Prince Jones (2000), Timothy Thomas (2001), Orlando Barlow (2003), Ousmane Zongo (2003), Alberta Spruill (2003), Timothy Stansbury (2004), Ronald Madison and James Brisette (2005), Henry Glover (2005),

Sean Bell (2006), DeAunta Terrell (2007), Tarika Wilson (2008), Oscar Grant (2009), Shem Walker (2009), Victor Steen (2009), Kiwane Carrington (2009), Aaron Campbell (2010), Steven Eugene Washington (2010), Aiyan Jones (2010), Danroy Henry (2010), Derrick Jones (2010), Reginald Doucet (2011), Reheim Brown (2011), Kenneth Harding (2011), Alonzo Ashley (2011), Kenneth Chamberlain (2011), Ramarley Graham (2012), Sgt. Manuel Loggins (2012), Raymond Allen(2012), Dante Price (2012), Nehemiah Dilard (2012), Wendell Allen (2012), Shereese Francis (2012), Kimani Gray (2013), Deion Fludd (2013), Miriam Carey (2013), Andy Lopez (20130, Jordan Baker (2014), Yvette Smith (2014) and many others have cast police departments into wrong light and even homeland security officers mandated with the responsibility of law and order enforcement being tagged "killer cops."

Are white Americans also being killed by black cops?

In the wake of increasing cases of police shooting African Americans whom they have more often labeled as criminals in possession of drugs or firearms, there has been a raging debate as to whether the converse is also true.

Do black cops kill whites? Or what level of threat do the victims pose to law enforcement officers who use deadly force in line of duty? Agreeably, not only minorities in the US have been targeted by killer cops, but there have also been many cases of black police officers killing or even wounding unarmed white civilians through gun shots. Further, despite the fact that findings that police in the United States of America has been trending for all the wrong reasons and that blacks have had their lives ended in the hands of cops who use deadly force, it has emerged that more whites have also been slain by killer cops. The fact that blacks of African and Hispanic origin are categorized as a minority is perhaps what has resulted in such explosive reactions worldwide. However, when the death rates attributed to legal interventions that end fatally are measured against the population of whites and black, interesting findings emerge.

The dark ages of blacks being enslaved in the west, including America, has not faded in many minds even today, and the descendants of those who were enslaved, tortured and made servants to white Americans live on American soil as proud Americans, thanks to the days of heightened civil rights activism that inspired the famous "I have dream rhetoric" by Martin Luther King Junior. American has a long standing history of racism and the recess of it is still engraved in the minds of many people who feel a certain race is inferior. From employment opportunities to economic opportunities, studies have laid bare a perceivable bitter past of blacks which is yet to be completely eradicated by recent economic reforms advocating for equal human rights protection and economic freedom. Also, judging from the facts and findings based on those who have been slain by police, a predictable pattern of defense is evident.

In most cases, wrongful use of deadly force has always been attributed to an allegedly illegal firearm ownership by those who have been shot and killed. The big question that many would be asking to this end is; what is the best thing to do to avoid being shot and killed if the alleged killer cops always find a line defense by alleging that the deceased victim was found with a gun or was charging at the cops with a weapon? Let's get closer to this by looking at gun violence and extra-judicial killings in the next chapter.

Chapter 2: Demystifying Gun Violence and Extra-judicial Killings.

Incidences of gun violence in the United States have left many dead and when statistics of cases that have passed without the notice of public watchdogs such as the media, gun violence is one of the leading causes of deaths in U.S.A. The question that many have been asking themselves is how best can these deadly incidences be prevented? Because tens of thousands have lost their lives through gun violence menace, the issue has received a widespread public outcry and the national as well state governments have been urged to take urgent measures that would see a reduction is loss of lives by putting in place measures to curb illegal ownership of firearms. The question is; could this be the main reason why police have in recent memory resolved to using deadly force because they always think a suspect could be in possession of a firearm hence a potential risk to life?

The Root Cause of the Problem: Gun Violence and the use of Deadly Force by Police.

In the year 2010, the United Nations Office on Drugs and Crime made alarming revelations in relations to gun violence and how the menace has resulted to a rise in crime from bank robberies, the killing of innocents, killing of cops and homicides. In its findings, it emerged that an estimated 67% of Americans are in possession of firearms either licensed or illegally particularly among the young adults. The rate at which these firearms are being misused is what has raised many eyebrows and event generated a widespread public debate both in the congress and outside. On many occasions, the congress has discussed and even passed legislations that seek to reduce cases of gun violence and most importantly control the number of guns in the hands of civilians.

You can imagine what situation it would be like when civilians own more guns and other firearms than the security forces that are mandated with the responsibility of protecting civilians. Two issues emerge out of this. It is either civilians or a section of the populace are growing increasingly impatient or suspicious of the police force or crime prevalence rates have overwhelmed the cops and civilians have decided to take the law in their own hands. In another instance, because the number of civilians owning guns is more than alarming and incidences of civilians carrying out mass shootings in public places still fresh in many minds, the police cannot trust a suspect. They always think whenever there is a 911 distress call, someone somewhere is armed and is likely causing havoc.

Instances of legal firearms holders brandishing or even drawing their guns and charging at law enforcement officers could be the likely cause of homeland security's perceived militarization. Perhaps this could be the only justification for use of deadly force. Whenever there is lack of restraint when handling a suspect, deadly force as used by cops has always resulted in the loss of lives. Incidentally, the notion that minorities in the U.S are prone to committing crimes like felony and dealing in hard drugs is said to be the reason why cops always resort to deadly force but again, the fact that minorities living in America have endured a long life of racial discrimination according to reports, makes their plight vulnerable and likely to elicit more public discussion despite the fact that their white counterparts are equally killed by cops who use deadly force.

Back to gun violence, in the same year of 2010, the United Nations Office on Drugs and Crime, in its findings, also indicated that gun violence resulted to more homicides than other causes. The deaths have either been attributed to a partner shooting another or self-inflicted gunshot. A report by the FBI on the same issue unearthed that 61% of gun violence are suicidal; meaning people taking their own lives using a firearm. The Federal Bureau of Investigation's findings released in the year 2012 indicated that at least 8500 homicides were firearms related. This was a reduction compared to FBI findings in the year 2010 which placed the figure at approximately 11,000.

Defining Gun Violence and Incidences of Gun Violence.

Any violence committed using a gun is called gun violence and it could take the form of mass shootings or armed robberies. Depending on the circumstances under which gun violence has been committed, it can be labeled as crime or not. Homicide is gun violence that is definitively a crime unless ruled justifiable. Other instances where gun violence is labeled as a crime include assaulting someone using a deadly weapon and suicide.

However, in cases where paramilitary, military or civilian use of guns causes unintentional or accidental injury, they do not fall under gun violence as a crime. Statistics obtained from Gun Policy Organization, which operates worldwide, place the number of guns owned by civilians at 75% which is an equivalent of 875 million guns. Only 25% percent of guns in use are owned and controlled by the government. The statistics further indicate that at least 1000 people are killed every day using a gun, globally.

A thin line then emerges between gun violence and use of deadly force or extra-judicial killings. Essentially, there is not any universally agreed upon definition of gun violence. Everything has been a speculation. However, the World Health organization defines gun violence as "an intentional application of physical power or force to threaten oneself or another person or a group and is likely to cause or result into injury, psychological harm, death, deprivation or maldevelopment is armed violence." This definition brings to the fore the issue of killer cops who have taken down tens of lives in the United States and other parts of the world.

Should killer cops be charged with homicide, gun violence as a crime or intentional armed assault?

What if the suspects who have since lost their lives at the hands of killer cops posed some kind of threats to the police in the likelihood that they were in possession of a gun? In the history of police killing civilians on suspicion that they are drawing a firearm to shoot at cops, innocent lives have been lost. There are however, few instances where the use of deadly force has largely been a justifiable homicide. It is also noteworthy that police have also lost their lives as a result of gun violence as a crime committed by fellow cops in mass shooting sprees or by civilians whose impatience with police has spiraled out of control.

Gun violence incidences like the Oikos University shooting, Aurora theatre shooting, Columbine high school massacre, Virginia Tech massacre, 2011 Tucson shooting and many others are still fresh in many minds and the gory tales of survivors and images of the slain, cast into light intentional gun violence as a deadly crime that many governments have yet to cope with. Perhaps what brings a sharper focus on the issue of gun violence as a serious crime are the mass shootings that have since taken place in many U.S schools, let alone the homicide cases of gun violence where hundreds of people have reportedly taken away their own lives.

The Sandy Hook Elementary School Shooting.

This is an incident that would probably be remembered in the memory of many U.S citizens as one of the worst criminal gun violence incidents that has taken place on U.S soil. In such a situation, a question emerges. What would have the cops done in the event that they arrived and found Adam Lanza still in the spree of fatal shootings of children and staff that ended up claiming the lives of 20 children and 6 staff members? Would the use of deadly force by cops be justifiable homicide therefore within the confines of legal provisions for self-defense?

Adam Lanza, on 14th December 2012 after shooting and killing his mother at home, drove into Sandy Hook Elementary School in Newton,

Connecticut upbeat for a shooting spree and fatally shot dead 20 children and 6 staff members.

The Sandy Hook School shootings remains the deadliest mass shooting in U.S history and the second deadliest shooting carried out by a single person after the 2007 Virginia Tech Shootings. As first responders arrived at the scene, Lanza shot himself on the head bringing the death toll to 27.

The aftermath of Sandy Hook School shooting prompted a heated debate in congress regarding gun control in the U.S.

Virginia Tech Massacre.

To date, the Virginia Tech Massacre remains the deadliest mass shooting in the U.S conducted by an individual. On April 16th 2007, Seung-Hui Cho who was a senior at the institute went on a shooting rampage that ended the lives of 32 people and wounded 17 others. The toll death was a culmination of two separate attacks by the same individual with one taking place at Virginia Polytechnic Institute and another one at State University at Blacksburg, Virginia. Six other people were injured while escaping through the windows. Medical reports indicated that Cho had at some point in time been diagnosed with anxiety disorder.

A question then comes to the fore, in the face of all these violent public mass shootings, what action are the police supposed to take to prevent more deaths? There have been indeed cases where police response has prevented more loss of life. Ranging from terrorists storming shopping malls and schools to civilians shooting aimlessly at people, some incidences have prompted cops to open fire on the terrorists or people engaged in armed assault and in the event preventing more loss of life.

While the plight of American minorities have been highlighted in incidences where innocent and unarmed civilians have been subjected to deadly force like the cases of Brown and Garner, the way one is supposed to act when confronted by homeland security forces has largely remained a raging debate.

Demystifying Extra-judicial Killings.

The term extra-judicial killings have remained elusive with regard to its meaning with many wrongly applying it in some contexts that are within the confines of legal provision.

What is an Extra-judicial killing?

Extra-judicial killings denote the use of deadly force by government apparatus such as the army or the police force. In most cases, extra-judicial killings are seen to target opposing political groupings, trade unionists, and dissenting people and activities. In most cases, they are never sanctioned by a judicial process because those who have committed the act are never brought to justice through an independent legal process.

Around the world and especially in places like Syria and Iraq, cases of extra-judicial killings have been making headlines when key and leading political elites are eliminated by the gunfire of an opposing camp. Other places where extra-judicial killings have made headlines for religious or political reasons include Yemen, Afghanistan, and Pakistan, parts of South America, Russia, the Philippines, and Bangladesh. At the center of extra-judicial killings, is the use of deadly force by the police and the armed forces have also featured prominently. Other people refer to extra-judicial killings as political or religious assassinations where an influential political elite or a radical religious scholar has been eliminated.

Are There Extra-judicial Killings in the United States?

In the United States, cases of extra-judicial killings have been largely attributed to killer cops killing unarmed civilians. This has more often than not brought to the fore and heightened debate on racism in America. One asks; is a killer Cop an extra-judicial killer?

The Case of Trayvon Martin Killed by Community Watch Member George Zimmerman.

The acquittal of George Zimmerman of a second degree murder charges brought to the fore the question of extra-judicial killings in America. While Trayvon Martin would go down in history as one of the many blacks in America whose deaths have brought to the fore the question of racial profiling, many questions remain unanswered; particularly with regard to the judicial processes in the United States which have largely been seen to favor police officers.

The death of Trayvon Martin elicited a public outcry especially among the black community and so did it bring to the public knowledge of an overt racism that continues to bedevil Americans despite the economic freedom and democratic rights in a country known to have the world's oldest and best written constitution. When a 911 operator told Zimmerman not follow Trayvon according to reports, he ignored and with utterances that were arguably racial, Zimmerman was set free. As one may ask, is the American judicial process so lenient when it comes to handing heavy penalties down to offenders and criminals or is racism part of the weakness? Well, the American population is largely constituted of the white majority who make up the bulk of the economic edifice but then the law provides for uplifting of minorities among who are African Americans.

Zimmerman's comments against Trayvon were threatening and after trailing Trayvon, the court's verdict which many described as largely pervasive and skewed on racial purposes found Zimmerman not guilty of killing Trayvon.

In a ruling that has since set Zimmerman free and the deceased Trayvon guilty, the court indicated that the accused acted in self-defense despite evidence that Trayvon was unarmed at the time of his death. Once again, the idea of a mass civil rights movement surfaced as was with the days of Luther King Jr.

This is probably one of the many incidences of police or law enforcement officers in the United

States who bring suspects under control using deadly force and in the process kill them. It is a case that has largely been described as extra-judicial killing in many quarters. Studies have established that one black American is killed by cops every 28 hours and the role of media in covering such incidents has largely been questioned save for the few cases that have elicited public protests.

Well, the debate on gun ownership is rampant in U.S and in many other countries around world the where religious, political and racial profiling has resulted in many innocent deaths. If we are to take a single instance like that of Trayvon, our findings and consequently conclusion will be largely skewed to justify the thinking and expectations of a certain group. However, as discussed in chapter one where a number of blacks have lost their lives thanks to killer cops, racial profiling in America and pervasive application of law gets a limelight. You would not want to incite racial emotions in a peace-loving people and even if the accused cops were justified in killing blacks in self-defense, all being set free still cast a dark shadow on the transparency of judicial processes in the United States.

If the targeted or profiled killings of terrorists would fit the bill of judicial killings America has undertaken outside its territory, then we would probably run out of numbers to count. In the face of resolving conflicts at home and abroad, American peacekeeping and homeland security forces have employed deadly force and in part, partaken in what would best fit the description of judicial killings. When the court pronounced George Zimmerman not guilty and declared Trayvon Martin guilty, widespread protests ensued. Many protesters carried placards that advocated for an end to racism and justice for Trayvon. It was a time of "Black Lives Matter."

Are Minority Killings in the U.S Racially Instigated or a Consequence of Law and Order Enforcement?

The killing of Michael Brown and Eric Garner by cops also aroused racial emotions and in the event, blacks who could not withhold their rage for long took to the streets demanding justice. To many, it was a case of racially profiled killings which however was not manifested in all the other cases of African Americans who have been shot by cops. The explosive reactions that followed the killing of Trayvon were in no way related to the application of deadly force against unarmed blacks but a clear advocacy for minority rights and an end to racism. In a show of solidarity among the black communities in the U.S following the death of Trayvon, many also took to the streets carrying placards that read 'I am Trayvon Martin.' This was undisputedly a powerful message that urged for action against racism.

The police officer who applied a chokehold on Eric Garner perhaps did not expect it would result in his death because to him it was just but a way of restraining Garner However, different accounts from the officers themselves and the public were an ideal example of a problem deeply rooted in America's system. While the cops said Garner was selling untaxed illegal cigarettes, eye witness accounts indicated that Garner was confronted by police after starting a public fight but could this have been a reason enough to have him killed? As for the case of Michael Brown whom police officer Daren Wilson said was looking like a demon when an altercation ensued between them in the police SUV, many interpreted the statement as racial and therefore would not have been a reason enough to fatally shoot Brown. Well, it is however noteworthy that there have been isolated cases of blacks whose criminal activities have resulted in inconsequential deaths when confronted by cops because when ordered to peacefully surrender they failed to do so. Down the history of America's struggle with racism, Trayvon's shooting would perhaps go down in many minds as a modern day extrajudicial killing that was racially inspired.

What is Law and Order Enforcement and Should Deadly Force be Used?

In every country around the world, citizens are required to conduct themselves in a manner that is in tandem with established laws. The constitution of any country enshrines prescribed codes of conduct that the citizenry is supposed to follow suit and when one fails to do so, it becomes a breach of law. Law breakers are therefore supposed to be subjected to formal punishments as prescribed by the constitution on the prescribed code of conduct or subjected to the judicial court process to determine if one is guilty or innocent. The question that one would be asking in this regard is that, did the likes of Eric Garner, Trayvon Martin and Michael Brown commit any crime and if so what would have been the right way to administer punishment as established by the law? The other question that has kept heads rolling even to date is what became of the police officers who took the lives of the aforementioned blacks with gunfire? Were they let to walk the streets freely or were they subjected to a fair trial and were justice served? These and many more questions are what chapter three would seek to answer in the most explicit way.

Defining Law Enforcement.

Law enforcement is largely an exercise of maintaining peace, order and unity among a people through a structured system. The members of society that act in a certain way to enforce law and maintain peace and order are referred to as the police and this they do through discovering incidences of law breaking, prevention of possible incidences of law breaking, punishing law breakers and even conducting rehabilitation for law breakers. It is noteworthy that not all law breakers are conscious of the act or offence they are committing and this calls upon the police to always act with caution because among suspected law breakers, there are those who are mentally ill and the best way to punish them is not through the application of deadly force during physical arrest but careful handling of a situation that may result into unprecedented death.

The deaths of African Americans have seen the black community accuse the police of using deadly force on even mentally ill suspects. Examples of African Americans who were said to be mentally ill but were shot and killed by the police include Ezell Ford and Kajieme Powell whose lives were ended in August 2014. This brings to the fore the question of how should the police handle mentally ill suspects when it comes to using force during arrest? Well, some mass shootings in U.S schools such as Sandy Hook Elementary School and Virginia Tech School brought forward intriguing findings. It was discovered that the suspects that stormed the institutions had some form of mental instability and this cast into light the question of how do firearms fall into wrong hands especially those of young adults who are mentally unstable. In most of the U.S shootings, either by police or young adults in public spaces like schools, there have been a good number of linkages with mental illness. The question is, despite some of those involved in these shooting taking their own lives, is it right to take the life of a mentally retarded suspect using a firearm as was with the case of shooting Ezell and Powell? Here, police have not only been publicly accused of using deadly force but also negligence which is largely unethical in the practice and one wonders how such cops are set free without any charges even when subjected to an intensive legal process involving a grand jury that reflects the faces of all the American communities.

In the keeping of law and order, self-defense is permissible in the event that the suspect is armed and dangerous. This brings us to another interesting issue that we shall discuss in chapter three. What is justifiable homicide? The U.S laws and especially the constitution which is the supreme law provides for lawful arrest and the manner in which the police is supposed to conduct an arrest. However, the manner in which the courts have been seen to subvert justice has continued to raise eyebrows even today.

This takes us back to the case of Trayvon Martin's case which many people, especially the blacks, waited with bated breath that justice was going to be served only for it to turn out that Martin's killer, who many people said acted in a racist manner when trailing Trayvon and finally shooting him, was set free

Chapter 3: Killer Cop and Legal Process: Justice or Injustice?

According to the United States Supreme law; the constitution, no one is entitled to take another person's life at will. The same law that protects civilians is the same that guarantees safety to security officers. Law breakers are therefore not immune to prosecution in the event that they commit a serious crime like taking another person's life. Even though Daren Wilson, the cop who killed Michael Brown resigned from New York Police Department, the legal process he was subjected to was largely seen as pervasive and skewed. Further, Daniel Pantaleo, the cop who shot Eric Garner is now free because he was never brought to justice. In the history of white cops killing African Americans, the trials of George Zimmerman and Daren Wilson saw that establishment of a grand jury at the very onset gave people false hope that the police officers would be brought to justice. However, after weeks of legal proceedings and intensive investigations, much was seen to have been swept under the carpet. The question that many asked is, is it right to kill an unarmed black man in the event that a cop fails to arrest him?

More questions that also touch on the way a suspect is supposed to behave during an arrest have also continued to feature prominently in public debates.

Legal Decision and Reactions Involving the Killing of Trayvon Martin.

The first question that anyone should be asking when it comes to the trial of George Zimmerman regarding the death of Trayvon Martin is; was justice fairly served and if so what procedure of legal inquiry was applied that eventually found Zimmerman not guilty of any criminal charges?

Stand your Ground Law

When Zimmerman was arrested, the police who arrived within two minutes of the shooting took him into custody and he was later treated for head injuries which were said to have been caused by a struggle between him and Trayvon. However, after being grilled for five hours, the police said that Zimmerman was immune to arrest and immune to further prosecution due to the stand your grand law statute. The question is; what does this law stipulate?

Well, the stand your ground law allows an individual to protect himself or herself and even defend oneself, own life or limb against a perceived danger even if it means using lethal force. Up to date, at least forty six U.S states have adopted the law and it has been used in making some of the landmark but unsatisfactory judgments involving the shooting of minorities. The question is, despite the bare evidence that Trayvon Martin did not pose any threat against Zimmerman because he was unarmed, how could it be possible to find the shooter not guilty of any charges? Does the U.S have laws that prosecute racial killings that have continued to take many innocent lives across different states because according to video footage, Zimmerman made utterances that could only be interpreted as racial profiling and which most likely led to trailing and eventually fatally shooting and killing Trayvon?

The trial of Zimmerman started on June 10th 2013 in Sanford. A month later; he was acquitted of any charges on July 13th 2013. The court sitting in Sanford ruled that Zimmerman was not guilty of second degree murder charges.

Martin who was shot on the 26th of February 2013 at night in Sanford, Florida U.S was a seventeen year old son to Sybrina Fulton and Tracy Martin. His parents got divorced in the year 1999. Martin was attending Dr. Michael M. Krop High School and was said to be living with his mother and an older brother in Miami's Florida Gardens.

When the trial of George Zimmerman began, a jury of jury of six female judges was constituted and during the trial process, the prosecution appeared inclined to stir up emotions in the jury by portraying Trayvon in the wrong light. The prosecution opened the court hearings by describing Trayvon as a hate-filled liar, a statement which was largely seen to echo Zimmerman's sentiments on the night he fatally shot and killed Trayvon. The proceedings then went on with the defense team producing evidence that would back Zimmerman and the law of stand your ground to the disadvantage of Trayvon. Pictures of blood dripping from the back of Zimmerman's head were displayed in court to justify that he acted in self-defense. That was to be day one of the trial. The trial went ahead to the second day with more evidence being tabled. At some point a bag of Skittles which were allegedly found in Trayvon's pocket were shown to the court. The court proceedings involved tabling of even a DNA test on scrapings found under Martin and Zimmerman's fingernails. Largely, all the evidence portrayed Trayvon as the aggressor and this eventually would set the accused free of any second degree murder charges. The question is, was justice fairly served, many argued it was not served on the basis of the fact that Trayvon Martin was harmless at the time of his killing. The events leading up to Martin's fatal shooting and judicial process decisions were largely seen as pervasive justice based on racial profiling in America's legal system.

The black community was and is still aggrieved even today. Zimmerman may not have come out as a killer Cop but the use of deadly force and extra-judicial killing became a subject of discussion.

The Trial of Daren Wilson Involving the Killing of Black Teenager Michael Brown.

The details of events leading up to the fatal shooting of Michael Brown are scanty compared to those surrounding Trayvon Martin's death but, the death altogether brought to the fore not just the perceived plight of African Americans but also highlighted the chilling cases of Killer Cops using deadly force against unarmed civilians.

After a largely opaque judicial process that acquitted Daren Wilson of any murder charges involving the alleged killing of Michael Brown, the family of the deceased decided to file a civil suit against the city of Ferguson. The case was filed under Missouri's wrongful death statute. Ferguson attorney said the evidence still remains the same except for presentations in line with the new suit which is largely civil and where Brown's family are seeking a compensation of $75,000 as punitive and compensatory damages which will be in excess of attorney's fees.

In an earlier suit, a grand jury declined to charge Daren Wilson of any charges citing that the police officer did not break any law relating to manslaughter and murder. According to news reports, Daren Wilson, the cop who shot and

killed Michael Brown, had not committed any murder. Brown and his friend were on 9th August stopped by Daren Wilson for jaywalking during which a struggle ensued. This is what eyewitnesses said but the police reports compromised everything.

National Government Stance on Brown's shooting by Daren Wilson.

The shooting and killing of Michael Brown saw the U.S president address the public through a White House press briefing during which he urged Ferguson protestors to look for constructive outlets for their anger and appealed for calm. However, the president's appeal failed to calm the situation in Missouri as violence and street protests escalated. The president went ahead to say that the killing of Brown was sure to

elicit some negative reactions that would be newsworthy for TV but cautioned that throwing bottles and smashing cars was not going to solve the underlying issue of mistrust and genuine problems that Africans Americans continue to face in the United States.

After the grand jury's decision, the president urged those who are still aggrieved with the ruling to accept jury's decision of not indicting Daren Wilson. Apparently avoiding divulging into the specifics of the case, president Obama further reminded protestors that America is founded on the rule of law and people should learn to cope with the jury's decision. However, the president was cognizant of the fact that there are real reasons for mistrust and cautioned that it would be wrong to "tamp that down or paper it over."

In what appeared to be echoes of a deeply rooted problem of racism in America's history, the president, despite acknowledging the tremendous steps the people of America have made in coping with racism, said that Ferguson protests are an American issue and that the minority communities are not making up the problems they are facing. He sought to clarify that the progress America has made towards coping with racism cannot be ignored by citing himself as a witness to that great change. The president's speech came amidst protests in Ferguson during which reports of business premises being looted and set on fire were on air. In New York City streets, which play host to the largest population of African Americans, protests had already broken out.

Michael Brown's killing also sparked protests as far away as Oakland, California where dozens of protestors were reported to have blocked traffic. In other areas like Los Angeles and Chicago, protests were largely peaceful.

Was the Grand Jury's Decision Based on the Use of Deadly Force?

In submissions made to the grand jury that tried Daren Wilson on the murder of Brown, it was asked to establish if Wilson was liable to any of the five charges he was accused of which ranged from first degree murder to involuntary manslaughter.

On the other hand, the family of Michael Brown did conduct an autopsy and found out that their son succumbed to at least six gunshots with two shots to the head. In a more shocking revelation, St. Louis count attorney McCulloch revealed that Daren's gun was fired at least 12 times during the struggle. The prosecutor said Wilson acted following a broadcast over police radio that matched Michael's attire to that of a robber who had reportedly broken into a grocery store.

The ruling not to indict Wilson saw Michael's parents express their profound shock at the jury's decision which they said had let the killer of their son go free. The jury's decision sparked fresh protests in Ferguson, Missouri during which a number of arrests were made. No mention of using deadly force was forthcoming during the landmark ruling. According to Missouri law, a police officer may shoot an individual who is reasonably feared to be armed or considered a serious threat to a cop or another person. A number of courts have also made rulings stating that police officers may shoot in the likely event that someone suspected of killing or having committed a grievous injury is fleeing and could potentially pose more such threats to other people. This brings to the fore a lot of debate.

The question is; Was Daren's Wilson's description that Brown looked like a demon during the struggle in the Police SUV used to justify the real threat he posed to the officer and if Brown was not armed, was the deadly force used against him permissible and how often have police officers been charged for using deadly force on unarmed civilians?

The aftermath of police shootings of unarmed civilians has largely been seen as a pervasive and skewed application of law. This is because virtually all the cases have seen the cops accused were not brought to judicial process to determine their innocence or set free after a decision by a grand jury. The cases discussed above mirror similar situations following the decisions of the courts on murder cases involving slaying people belonging to America's minority races whose names were discussed or outlined in chapter one.

Chapter 4: Unraveling the truth: Perpetual Racism or Racial Disenfranchisement.

Going back to the time in America's history when racism was rife and in progress in many lives, it cannot be ignored that the same is still deeply rooted in the American system. Going by President Obama's comments in the aftermath of Michael Brown's murder, it is as much as American people have over the years learnt to embrace each other regardless of race, the complaints that have been forwarded by minority communities after killer cops murdered allegedly unarmed civilians are not made up.

The run up to the 1950s in the history of the United States of America saw heightened racist practices. Racism was clearly manifested in places like the military where there were essentially two separate units designed for the whites and the blacks. However the black military units were headed by whites. This could be a background to the claims that African Americans have always laid complaints using black cards which read "black lives matter" during public protests whenever one of their own is killed by a cop.

Simply defined, racism involves discrimination based on the color of one's skin and in the history of America during which it has struggled with racism, racist acts clearly manifested not just in the military as earlier mentioned, but also in the way people had access to social amenities like hospitals and public utilities like transportation. Essentially, the separation of hospitals and buses designated for whites and colored races was a clear manifestation in other parts of the world like Canada and United Kingdom during the era of slave trade. Even in places for drinking water, people witnessed hyper racial segregation. This was however to come to end with the enactment of the Civil Rights Act of 1875 following the fifteenth amendment to the constitution of the United States in 1870. This brought to the fore reconstruction efforts to end racism which further allowed minority races to exercise their democratic space by voting in elections to elect leaders of their choice. However, disenfranchisement still existed among minority races in 1890s.

Why were Michael Brown's, Eric Garner and Trayvon Martin's Deaths Such a Big Concern to the Minority Communities in America?

The killing of blacks by cops in the United States has not escaped the public limelight. In light of this, recesses of racism still exist in America as was echoed in President Obama's sentiments following the murder of Michael Brown when it was noted that America has made tremendous steps towards living in unity but indicated that the protests in Ferguson by the black community were not made up and that as much as the minority communities may feel aggrieved, they should seek better avenues and means of solving their problem.

What is Justifiable Homicide and Does it Qualify the Acquittal of a Killer Cop?

Justifiable homicide was said to be the case with Eric Garner's death after cop Pantaleo place a chokehold on his neck which eventually caused his death. The decision of justifiable homicide that saw Pantaleo not being brought to justice was arrived at following medical examinations results that were conducted by a New York based examiner who told Garner's family that their son died from homicide.

Well, justifiable homicide is enshrined in the U.S criminal law and is a concept that revolves around excuse, justification and exculpation. The law states that there are circumstances where homicide is justified when it is in view of events leading to it; harm was posed to an innocent person. In a court of law, the application of justifiable homicide must be proven using adequate evidence beyond any reasonable doubt. There are many other incidences or situations where police have used deadly force but the law could not bring them to justice due to the case being labeled as justifiable homicide.

Does U.S Law Allow the Police to Use Deadly Force Against Suspects?

Many people have been killed around the world by police gunfire. These incidents have taken place in varying circumstances ranging from pursuing a suspected criminal who is shot in the process of arrest, quelling violence during political upheavals to settling domestic problems. In the United States, while there are incidences where the use of deadly force has been excused especially in situations where a wanted criminal resists arrest, other scenarios have elicited widespread criticisms of racial profiling. A case in point is that of Eric Garner and Trayvon Martin. The question is, does deadly force refer to shooting to kill a suspect or there is a better interpretation to it?

A number of times, you must have come across signposts indicating that certain areas are restricted and that no unauthorized persons are allowed to get through unless with the permission of an installed commander. Then the sign post goes ahead to warn that the use of deadly force is allowed in such places should one fail to adhere to the rules or refuse an arbitrary search. Such are the signs which are phenomenal with military bases, isolated secret operation facilities and surveillance centers where the application of deadly force is permitted. But what about the use of deadly force in day to day law and order enforcement by police officers? What does the U.S law stipulate on this?

According to the United States Armed Forces definition of deadly force, it denotes that force which an individual uses, causes or that is known to a person or which a person should know would create a reasonable risk that could potentially cause death, injury or serious bodily harm. In most legal applications of deadly force, it ought to be and perhaps is justified in situations where it is of extreme necessity or as a last resort where an earlier means employed has less effects or when there is no other means apart from deadly force. Weapons that are likely to cause deadly force include bladed weapons, firearms, vehicles and explosives. This therefore brings to the fore a controversial question, should the police respond with deadly force in circumstances where a suspect is in possession of the weapons earmarked as likely to cause deadly force? But again, what one would want to ask is that did the police that have since been marked as "killer cops" for slaying the likes of Garner, Brown, Powel and Parker reached that extreme necessity where the application of deadly force was the only option? Simply put, did the actions of officer Pantaleo, Zimmerman and Wilson meet the prescription of applying deadly force or were their actions racially instigated?

It was alleged that Powell who died at the hands of a "killer Cop" had a knife but no evidence has come forth to back such claims. In the case of Garner and Michael Brown, no weapon was discovered that linked them to being dangerous to the lives of the police. This gives rise to another question; does failure to adhere to police orders in the event of arrest such as raising one's hands call for the use of deadly force?

These are questions whose answers have been elusive but in cases of justifiable homicides, a jury is likely to rule in favor of the police. For example, if a suspect was on a shooting spree that would take away many innocent lives, then, such a person would prompt the police to use gunfire on him or her to prevent casualties.

Accusations that have been leveled against Killer Cops taking innocent lives are not something that is only reserved for the United States but it happens elsewhere and in almost all countries around the world. There have been reports of extra-judicial killings that fit the perfect definition of deadly force. In countries where police have been dispatched to quell violence during political upheavals, protestors have responded by throwing projectiles at the cops and this begs the question, what do a country's laws and the constitution stipulate when it comes to defining the use of a weapon that is likely to force the police to use deadly force during law and order enforcement?

Above all, in the event that a suspected criminal is confronted by the police, how is one supposed to act or behave to avoid an incident of a "killer cop" coming up? We look at this in the next chapter.

Chapter 5: Safety Precautions: How to Avoid being shot-Dos and Don'ts.

Well, the law in some of its universal provisions stipulates that one is not guilty until proven so. This is something applicable in any part of the world. Police can always make an arrest and present suspects before a court of law but this does not mean the suspect is guilty. Their main duty in any part of the world is to maintain law and order. They enforce this by arresting suspected law breakers. The key point that underscores everything from the time of arrest to the time one is being presented before a jury or a court of law is the term "suspect." Being suspected of any wrong doing does mean you have actually committed the alleged offense. Even during a court hearing, one is presumed innocent unless proved guilty through objective evidence, unbiased truth and investigations, and independent judgment. The question is; why do some suspects opt to run away from the police when ordered to surrender because this has always forced cops to use deadly force? There have been coincidences where an innocent person has perfectly fit the description of an alleged offender being pursued.

Taking two cases discussed in chapter one, pressman Dante Parker was mistaken for a fleeing suspect which a 911 call had described as escaping on a bicycle. On arrival at the scene in San Bernardino County in California, cops mistook Dante Parker for the alleged burglar fleeing on a bike. A struggle was reported to have ensued during which another case of "killer cop" become a public debate. The same happened in the case of Kajieme Powell whom a 911 call had described as having stolen. This was later to emerge as misreporting because no stolen items were found in his pockets. The St. Louis Police Chief and the arresting police were sued for wrongful death by Powell's family. Justice is yet to be served. This brings to the fore another big question, do the police departments always dispatch arresting officers with the right information?

There have also been cases of the public making a 911 call on false premises and later recanting their statements. A case in point is Crawford's killing discussed in chapter one which took place in Ohio's Wal-Mart. Ronald Ritchie who called the police and said Crawford was carrying a gun and pointing at people with it was to retract his account a month later when he said Crawford was not pointing at people with a gun in the Ohio Wal-Mart. In many other cases where police have responded to distress calls in homes only to shoot and kill the wrong person only point at the legal and law enforcement discrepancies that exist anywhere in the world. They could be a pointer to racial profiling but again, acting on misinformation would always lead to unintended casualties.

How to Respond During an Arrest and Avoid Being Shot.

Coming under arrest of policing forces has seen successful and nasty ends in equal measures as far law and order enforcement is concerned. Deadly force at the scene of a crime has seen suspects killed but again, there have also been countless incidences of peaceful arrests. Police reports as pertains to the minority police shootings in America have indicated that the suspects either tried to flee, fight or struggle and in that event, a cop had to pull the trigger. How are you supposed to avoid this?

- **Raise your hands up**

The increasing cases of gun violence have consequently seen policing forces put their lives on the line during patrols or when called upon to salvage a situation. Such are the situations that see cops run into a deadly criminal brandishing a weapon whom is likely to shoot back. This is why in the event of arrest, when a suspect acts in a manner suggestive of being in possession of a weapon, cops will always order them to put their hands up where they can see them to prevent the likelihood of the suspect drawing a weapon. Well, the best thing you can do is to adhere and do as ordered. You will most definitely not be shot.

- **Do Not Run from the Police**

Fleeing from the police when ordered to stand still, lie down or raise your hands up is gambling with your life. Chances are the police will assume you are a runaway deadly criminal and shoot to demobilize or to kill you.

No one, except for a suicide bomber, wants to lose his or her life so easily but despite the fact that everyone is growing uneasy with the "killer cop" incidences, the best thing to do during arrest is do as ordered by the police.

- **Does Not Physically engage or Struggle with the Police (surrender).**

Resisting arrest angers and irritates the police. It is a furtherance of a peace violation and breaking the law even more. To avoid the likelihood of being shot by the cops, the best thing to do is surrender and let the law takes its course. The law is there to protect everyone and struggling with the police is a show of guilt which they would likely use to gauge you as a threat and perhaps shoot to kill in self-defense or press more charges against you in a court of law.

- **Do Not Argue**

Everyone deserves a fair trial and the law guarantees this through the provision of innocent until proven guilty. In the event that a suspect argues with the police in way that is likely to be termed obscenity, the arresting police could get angry and fire a shot because they would treat you as a hostile criminal but not as a suspect. The law will protect them on the basis of the stand your ground statute or justifiable use of deadly force. The best thing you can do when the police want to arrest you is let them handcuff you and take you to the station knowing truth will always set you free.

- **Do what you are Told (obey police orders).**

Disobedience of police orders is likely to cause you trouble which could include being shot to demobilize you. As long as you are a labeled a suspect by the police, they have the right to frisk you. This is meant to clear any suspicions they could have against you and disobeying orders will fuel and confirm their doubt making shooting you the most likely outcome.

- **Agree to be Handcuffed**

By agreeing to be handcuffed, you confirm to the law and order enforcement officers you are a law-abiding citizen. However, resisting would be used as evidence against you or lead to a situation whereby you are shot. In case of injuries, let the cops know in advance so that you are not hurt in the process of being handcuffed. Encounters with the police are likely to degenerate into a brawl and even occasion the use of deadly force if a suspect resists arrest. It is better you remain calm even if you are innocent.

- **Respect the Police and Refrain from Issuing Threats**

From the onset of an arrest, even if you know you have done nothing wrong, do not hurl insults at the police. They not only enforce law and order but also represent it. Threatening a cop will make things worse for you and make you a person of questionable character. Everyone is entitled to an attorney and ensure you ask for one by the time you have arrived at the police station if the arrest will see you detained.